The Deep, Green Sea

by Josh Weinstein
illustrations by Shelley Dieterichs

Harcourt Brace & Company

Orlando Atlanta Austin Boston San Francisco Chicago Dallas New York Toronto London

This is the sea, the deep, green sea.

This is the gleaming beach by the deep, green sea.

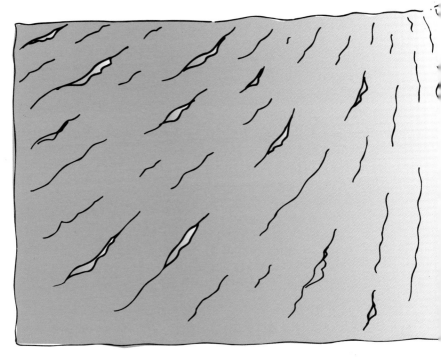

3

This is a tree leaning in the breeze on the gleaming beach by the deep, green sea.

This is a neat seat beneath
the tree on the gleaming beach
by the deep, green sea.

This is Jean Lee dreaming
in the heat on the neat seat
beneath the tree
on the gleaming beach
by the deep, green sea.

This is a sweet peach that
Jean Lee eats on the neat seat
beneath the tree
on the gleaming beach
by the deep, green sea.

These are the bees
that see the sweet peach
that Jean Lee eats
on the neat seat
beneath the tree
on the gleaming beach
by the deep, green sea.

This is Jean Lee when she sees the bees coming after the sweet peach!

These are Jean Lee's feet when
she leaps out of the neat seat
beneath the tree and . . .

runs down the beach
to the deep, green sea.

11

This is Jean Lee in the sea,
the deep, green sea.
If you need Jean Lee,
this is where she'll be!